ISBN 978-0-259-43045-2
PIBN 10816842

For support please visit www.forgottenbooks.com

1 MONTH OF
FREE
READING

at
www.ForgottenBooks.com

By purchasing this book you are eligible for one month membership to ForgottenBooks.com, giving you unlimited access to our entire collection of over 1,000,000 titles via our web site and mobile apps.

To claim your free month visit:
www.forgottenbooks.com/free816842

English
Français
Deutsche
Italiano
Español
Português

www.forgottenbooks.com

Mythology Photography **Fiction**
Fishing Christianity **Art** Cooking
Essays Buddhism Freemasonry
Medicine **Biology** Music **Ancient**
Egypt Evolution Carpentry Physics
Dance Geology **Mathematics** Fitness
Shakespeare **Folklore** Yoga Marketing
Confidence Immortality Biographies
Poetry **Psychology** Witchcraft
Electronics Chemistry History **Law**
Accounting **Philosophy** Anthropology
Alchemy Drama Quantum Mechanics
Atheism Sexual Health **Ancient History**
Entrepreneurship Languages Sport
Paleontology Needlework Islam
Metaphysics Investment Archaeology
Parenting Statistics Criminology
Motivational

MAN

A STUDY

BY

ALBERT EDWIN CLATTENBURG, B.D.

*Vicar of Christ Church, Christiana Hundred, and
Immanuel Church, Wilmington, Delaware.*

ARTI et VERITATI

BOSTON: RICHARD G. BADGER
THE COPP CLARK CO., LIMITED, TORONTO

THE GORHAM PRESS BOSTON, U. S. A·

DEDICATION

To all those saints,
alive and dead,
who have opened up
to me the vision that
I have of God and man
this book is humbly dedicated.

FOREWORD

ONLY the fact that other men's thoughts have helped me to gain a better view of the things that pertain unto the real life of man permits me to send into the world this Book. Nothing new is sought, only a resetting of truths that may be seen by all who seek. It is not primarily intended to convert unbelievers to our Lord and Saviour, and the life which He revealed; rather it is an attempt to stir up the believers sufficiently so that they will go out and do the converting work. Upon those who now know the last command of Christ, "Go ye into all the world and preach the Gospel to every creature," devolves the carrying out of the command. It is with the hope that more "who know" may be prompted to become one with the group "who do" that the writer dares to send forth these thoughts.

Purposely quotations from the Bible have been avoided for four reasons:—

Firstly. That the work may not seem to be exegetical or expository.

Secondly. That "the man in the street" who

may also be "a man in the Church" may feel
that he too has the opportunity to reach the
conclusions arrived at. If a technical knowledge of the Holy Scriptures were evident, he
would feel that he had no part or lot in the
work.

Thirdly. That controversy may not be possible by reason of the fixing of interpretation to
any part of God's Word.

Fourthly. That the writer might not be compelled to become dogmatic, or to seem to base
any of his arguments on the traditional sources
or beliefs of the Christian Church.

The author recognizes fully that the same
reasons may be urged as cause for adverse criti-
cism. He as fully recognizes that a certain
group of people will imagine this Book to be a
sanction of the current thought—"A man's conduct is that by which he should be judged; if
he is what the world calls good, he is all that
he should be."

It is necessary, if a man will realize the highest position in this life and in the life to come,
THAT HE BELIEVE THAT JESUS
CHRIST IS GOD. For it is granted only to
such believers to know the highest possible life;
and only to beings holding this belief is granted

the power to make it actual in the world. With those who try to minimize "the faith," in order to gain converts, the writer would see all men embracing the Religion of Christ. The Religion of Christ must remain constant, however, else those embracing it, and those coming to embrace it, will be found with no lamp burning when the Bridegroom comes.

St. Andrew's Day, 1913.   A. E. C.

CONTENTS

CONTENTS

"*Many of Darwin's followers and expounders have gone to extreme lengths in their assertions. Not only do they assert, with a positiveness of which Darwin was never guilty, that species have had a common origin through natural causes, but that all organic beings had been equally independent of supernatural forces. It is a small thing that two species of elephant should have descended from a common stock. Nothing will satisfy them but to assert that the elephant, the lion, the bear, the mouse, the kangaroo, the whale, the shark, the shad, birds of every description—indeed, all forms of animal life, including the oyster and the snail—have arisen by strictly natural processes from some minute speck of life, which originated in far distant time.*"

MAN—HOW CAME HE TO BE HERE?

CHAPTER I

MAN—HOW CAME HE TO BE HERE?

THE greatest subject that man can study is man himself. He who takes up the study of inanimate things may have a very attractive and interesting work, but sooner or later he will know enough about those things to satisfy him. And enough to qualify as an expert along those lines. The same may be said of those who study living things other than man himself. Ornithology, Botany, Zoology, or Piscatology, attractive and interesting as they are singly or collectively, can give man only a larger knowledge of living things outside of himself. The study of man not only gives man a greater knowledge of humanity, but also opens up to him a larger vision of the world in which he lives, gives him a deeper insight into the life to be led in it, and eventuates in a higher personal aim and service. All seekers after knowledge that falls short of humanity finally come to a place where they are satisfied with the results attained. Give a man the love of study, and make the object of his study man, and you have started something that can end only with the earthly life of the student.

Man—from whence is he? It is most interesting to visit a Zoological Garden and find there, in the faces, forms, and actions of the shut-in fishes, animals, and birds, reminders of men whom we have met. It is just as interesting to read books that would trace man's pilgrimage from the fish life, through the animal life, until at last he comes upon the scene as man. We can see similarities in the life of man to events that transpire in the life of fishes, animals, and birds. Does that fact necessarily teach us that man ascended from such life? Does it not teach us just as surely, and without any stretch of our imagination, in order that the decided "breaks" in the line may be accounted for, that the same Power that caused the fishes, animals, and birds to be, caused man also to be? Is there not in the evident resemblances an argument for the unity of all creation, a unity that demands a Unifying Creator? We feel, it must be instinctively, when we look at creatures that reveal characteristics almost human, that man has been the product of a Mind, and that Mind, when creating man, intended to produce a being that would be the head of all created beings and things upon earth. Do you suppose that any human being, picture the most crude human you can imagine, when looking at a baboon would think that only the question of time separated the looker from the looked-at? In fanciful moments, yes; but not when sane and sober. Such an evolution came from an abnormal mind. Man, when reasoning from facts known to facts unknown, is apt to go the wrong way. Man has been led astray by his fancies when trying to make present facts account for unknown facts. We are at liberty to suppose that man did take a wrong step when he anounced the hypothesis that man came up through the animal or brute world from the world of the jelly-fish.

No one would dare deny the quite apparent fact that the mighty oak comes from the insignificant acorn. That which is in a thing may be produced from that thing. (The magician's wonderful hat at one time contained the quantity of things that the magician takes from it. That these things evolved from the hat itself no one seems to claim.) The fact that jelly-fishes are not progressing through the animal world into the world of humanity to-day seems proof positive that man is not, at this time, potentially in the jelly-fish. We expect from a seed or egg, by reason of our long experience with seeds and eggs, that which is in the seed or egg. We do not expect to raise grapes from thorn seeds, nor figs from thistle seeds. That which is in each seed we expect to evolve from the seed, under the proper conditions. Under the hand of man anomalous growths may be cultivated. We may pluck thistles and figs from the same plant even though we may never raise one from the seed of the other. We likewise may graft the skin of a bear onto a man without changing the life principle of one into that of the other.

What good is really accomplished by imagining that the Creator of all rolled up into a tight ball the finest part of His creation and carefully placed the most insignificant part of His creation on the outside, the whole to be unwound only after a long term of years? Is it that we may congratulate ourselves on our smartness in finding out the Creator's method? Will any one deny His ability to do otherwise? There seems to be in the human being a distinct feeling that there is a Power above the power of the biggest and strongest man; and it seems to be very generally believed that that Power belongs to the Being who made all that we see. If that Being made all that we see, He must have had great Power. Did He have power enough to make man instantaneously, or must He bring life in its lowest form up to a certain standard before man could appear? To take up a thought that may put this clear: Was the magician compelled by force of circumstances to take out of the hat the great quantity of little things before he could bring to your gaze the great big thing? You will say no, he had power to do the last thing first, if he so willed. Is it therefore sensible for us to imagine a long laborious work for the Creator when He could in an instant of time do it all?

Of course the Creator could have placed man here on the earth just as the evolutionary theory says He did. How much simpler it makes the matter though, if we believe that the Creator, in due time, made man as man. It seems possible that the Creator could do either one or the other. Both methods demand a Creator with great Power. It is possible to say to-day, without much fear of contradiction, that man is here in the world by the will of the Life Giver. This cannot be taken away from us no matter how learned science may become. Scientists come to definite halting places; it is not given to man no matter how intelligent he may become, or how full he may store his mind with what the world calls knowledge, to know everything. He who made all reserves some things for Himself to know, and a truth is reserved for each age and time. Man may know from whence he is, for he may know the Father of all creation. The existence of a Life Giver, from whom all life has come, is one of the basal facts of knowledge.

Man is on the earth because the Life Giver willed, and caused, him to be here. The study of Comparative Anatomy may lead men to posit certain ideas, such for instance as man's gradual ascent from the animal world, but the truth of that posited statement has not yet been proven. Philosophies have tried to solve the problem of man's presence in the world, the whence, and why, but they have failed in some part. Embryologists may speculate from known facts about animals to unknown facts about man without proving that man is a lineal descendant of the ape. The study of man, confined to man himself, leads one to believe conclusively that man was caused to be with all the powers that are now his. Life in human form, like life in any form, is a gift from the Life Giver. Man is here in the world because a Power, above the great power of man, willed him to be.

You will find almost every philosophy known to history in the minds of the men with whom you associate. You will also find philosophies in your contact with men that are not easily labeled; individualistic, caused to be by reason of the emphasis that the one holding it has put upon some phase of the world or of life. The consensus of opinion among men, however, men who have used their minds enough to get any philosophical view of human life whatever, is that man is on the earth because the Power that gives life wishes him to be here. A great majority of the thinking men of every age place their presence in the world of men as an act of the Life Giver, and the whole race of men, from the beginning of human society to our time, as a definite act of the Creator, who wanted on the earth a being competent to act in harmony with Himself.

MAN'S POSSIBILITIES

CHAPTER II

MAN'S POSSIBILITIES

TO know man and his possibilities man must be studied all the time. Every day brings under man's power some new phase of an old force, or some new use of the created things already discovered. And it is not sufficient to take one man off into a far corner of the world and make an intimate study of him. One's study must be made in the world of men. The daily walk in and out among men of different classes in life, of different temperaments, must be adhered to, if one is to get the material from which to draw conclusions in the study of man.

The man who is outside of the daily life of ordinary men cannot study man in his normal life. That is why so many of our well meaning reformers make so many mistakes in their work of reforming. They know men in the abstract, what they are capable of being, and not in the concrete, as they actually are. Man must be among men, when at work, when at play, when tired and fretted by failure, and when rejoicing in the thought of deeds well done. Man must not expect to know man, if he himself has not been with men in all the circumstances that man is capable of bringing upon himself. The dreamer cannot know the acute man of business, unless by daily contact with him he comes to know him. The acute business man cannot know the dreamer unless by the same daily contact he is forced to know him. The lazy man cannot comprehend the man of unmitigated energy. Nor can the constant worker see the point of view of the indolent man. Man must know well all these different characters to appreciate each point of view. He need not necessarily be all of them, but his knowledge of them must be of the most intimate character. He must know the experience, the thoughts, hopes, and desires of all, if he is to look truly into the life of all. The man who laughs may also be capable of weeping, but no one knows that he can do so until he does. The melancholy man may have the reverse said of him. The only way to determine the possibilities of man is to mingle freely among men. To study them, not as curiosities, but as beings identical in kind with self, and worthy of as much consideration as we are willing to give to self.

Having secured the field for study what do we find there in the nature of possibilities that we may credit to man? As we walk up and down the world, and in and out in our daily life, we find very little that has not been touched by man's hand or mind. Man has a power within him which enables him to see what is, and further, prompts him to make it contribute to his own purpose. Instead of having a piece of matter weighing one hundred and fifty pounds, more or less, gifted with the ability to walk in and out in a daily search for food, we have a being that is capable of building up material things into forms that cannot be appreciated by the creatures whose sole ability is seen in their power to persist in being, and to reproduce creatures like themselves. Man is not to be compared with other lumps of matter simply because he has in his physical make-up the elements that are found in lumps of matter. He is not to be compared with the lower forms of life simply because his mode of existence is continued by reason of the food which he must, like them, take into his body. Man is made up, physically, of the elements that are common to all creation; he is also animate, and must receive nourishment in order to retain that characteristic; yet there is some added thing in man that is not found in the elements, as such; or by all animate creatures, as such. Thus we find in man two characteristics that are common to animate creation; one common to all creation; and still man stands apart from all other created things or beings by reason of the main characteristic, found alone in him, which sets him off from all other worldly things.

The atom and the molecule have dissolved into other terms. The scientific basis of the elements may change yearly (in name as well as in structure or action), yet man remains the same being, capable of the same action that has been his right from the beginning of what we call human life. The vortices may whirl, and other theories spring up in human minds to confute knowledge now dominant, but to have this so man must remain a being to do things forever.

Man is the one who is doing the revising. Man made terms and names are being discarded and new ones made daily. Man reasons out theories that are but stepping stones to higher ground. He says this to-day in order that he may say something else to-morrow. Each step in advance does away with the old position. In the midst of all this it is well to remember that

man is doing it all. Man must find out things.
He does find out things. He has more power
than an ordinary piece of matter. He has more
in his make-up than the highest type of animal
known to man. He may stand in the perfect-
ness of his manhood and look about him for
the reasons why such a thing is so, and why another thing is different. He may show to the
on-looker daily that he is a being different in
kind from any other created thing in the world.
This difference must be because of a special gift
not held in common with any other creature.
Matter and life he shares with all animate creation. The elements that go to make up the
world itself are found in him. The actions of
man reveal to the world a still higher characteristic than mere matter and life; they reveal the
vast power that man has over both those characteristics. Man is capable of controlling and
directing the things which we see. Energized
matter, or matter with potential energy, may
seem to have the same power to act. We realize the difference between it and man so soon as
the stored up energy is spent. We find the once
animate mass cold and lifeless. Man has forever in him this ability to reveal life, to do
things that require intelligence in the actor. Man

is for all time an energized being. When he seems to have lost this power to do things, by reason of the absence of the life principle, he ceases to be man, he has become a corpse. This permanent power over all creation sets man off from all other created beings on the earth. The radio-centric part of man is a different thing from the radio-centric part of mere matter. The non-checkable changes in the physical part of man cannot take away, or alter materially, that hidden mysterious power which sets him off from all other created beings.

The power of creation is man's. His possibilities are summed up in that sentence. Man may put life, energy, into inanimate objects; and new life into animate creation. If you have not seen man's child, an intricate machine, going through its appointed movements, turning out a newspaper ready for the street, you have not seen to any extent the possibilities of man. If you have not heard the perfected machine reproducing the voice and song of the world's best singers, you are not in touch with the powers of man. Man may take the roughest lump from the mine, the one that held out the smallest promise to the novice, and bring it back resplendent with the glory that only the Creator could make possible. Man's possibilities and powers fall not far short of the Life Giver himself. The Life Giver stands out from the world because of His vast Power over as well as in the world; man, the highest creation on the world's surface, stands out from all else because of his vast power over all things in the world. With the Creator all things are possible; with man, all things, save the bringing into being of something that never existed potentially, or the creating of independent life, are possible. Man not only names the other parts of creation, and the other creatures that exist, but also is able to bring all things to serve him, and to change the variety of all other created things by judicious reasoning and action.

The power or possibility that surmounts all other powers and possibilities in man, however, is the possibility of self-development. This is concretely revealed to the world by inner knowledge of self, and outward expression of self. Man, while busy with things other than himself, may reveal great possibilities and powers, but it is when he takes himself as the object of his study, and the thing to be perfected, that he shows the greatest possibility of all.

MAN'S CHIEF CHARACTERISTIC

CHAPTER III

MAN'S CHIEF CHARACTERISTIC

MAN'S power to control himself under any circumstances is the greatest gift that he evidences. This power is so called because it is one of the last powers realized. Man comes up from infancy and youth, using, as he progresses, all of his powers. He shows through them all the first power noticed, the power that prompts him to strive to satisfy his desires. And he exerts himself to the utmost in order to keep content the inner man. The child has been known to so exert itself in this attempt to get what it wanted that it brought upon itself instant death. Pulling the cloth under a lighted lamp has caused the death of many infants. The youth has been known to go bravely to his death when his highest aim was to see upon his school or academy walls a trophy won on the football field. The full grown man has gone down into the gutter and into Hell because he would have the drink that his inner desires craved.

The animal is not expected to exhibit more

intelligence, or as much, as man. Yet you will find the escaped fish quite wary when the hook is proffered the second time. The trusting kitten does not take food into its mouth hastily from the hand that has once given it something that was found unpalatable. Unlike man the animal averts in the second instance that experience which has been found to have been disagreeable or disappointing. This fact alone would not make us say that animals make up a world that is higher than the world of man. The animal, in the first instance, follows its desires when the man, without previous experience in that immediate field, could predict disappointment for the animal. The seeming virtue, or higher intelligence, in the animal, in that it does not allow itself to become subject to a second disappointment, is not sufficient to place the animal in a class higher than that occupied by man. It shows, however, that man must have stronger impulses or desires than those incident to the animal life. Having stronger impulses or desires, it takes a stronger power to control them. When man has desires of the animal class, multiplied to the intensity that they can be in man, it is a more difficult battle that he wages when he endeavors to make his body give up those desires. The animal stops to see if the conditions are the same as when the disappointment or disagreeable experience came in the previous instance. If the conditions look the same, the animal turns off in another direction. The desire is put aside. Man, instead, having within him an intense longing to do the contemplated thing, persists in doing it even in the face of the knowledge that the result cannot be other than disappointing and harmful. He goes near, sees clearly that the experience is to be exactly the same as before, and his desire is so strong that it makes him repeat the performance that proved once to be of no worth to him or to anyone else in the world.

When man begins to assert the power which he has, potentially, over his body, then he puts into being the highest power that he possesses. As you meet men daily you group them into two classes; those who have learned to exert this power; and those who have not yet learned to exert it. You will find yourself picking out men whom you know who seem, at all times, to have themselves in command; and men who are always getting themselves and others into trouble because they have not, at all times, themselves in command. You are helped in your seeking

after knowledge of these two classes by a study
of yourself. You see how easy it is to give way
to sudden impulses, and to yield to ardent desires. You find that there are times when, to
gain the object you have in view, you would do
almost anything. And the object in view may
have no connection whatever with what may
be called your higher life. When you have se-
sured the mastery of yourself the first time you
are made aware of a new life that is possible
for you. You then see that the body, yes, the
whole man, is safer when ruled by the thinking
part than when under the dominion of the flesh.

To give way to passion seems the easiest thing
that man does, if one may judge from the frequency of such action. To indulge the appetites
of man seems no difficult task. The whole of
man's life is a warfare between what is called
good in him and what is called bad. He inclines
toward what is bad, yet he has what may be
called a leaning toward the good. The highest
good that can come to man by his own act is to
get himself under the control of the real man in
him. Such control to be evident at all times.
We know that to achieve temporary control not
much power is demanded. The drunkard has
his moments of sobriety when he solemnly vows

that he will never touch a drop of intoxicating liquor. The roué has his moments, when, touched by the meanness of his recent act, he vows that he will keep his passions within due bounds. It is the man who controls himself under all circumstances who exhibits to the world the highest power that man has within him. Not one lapse in act; there may be desires to do so, for there would be no virtue in self control, if there were not desires and impulses to resist. We cannot expect man to become so holy that fleshly thoughts and fleshly desires would flee from him. It is because this controlling power over self is exerted in a world that prompts man to commit certain acts that are harmful to, himself and others that the power looms so large before our eyes. Place a man in the midst of every day life and temptation, it is the power within him that keeps him from yielding to the ever insistent call of his fleshly desires that calls forth our wonder and our admiration. It is the greatest power in the province of man. It is the power that reveals the presence of the master. The fact that such men can be found in organized society is warrant for the assumption that all men may reveal this power to the world. The sight of such a man should be inspiration enough to make beholders strive for the same position. It shows a higher ideal of life and manhood than is ordinarily held by man. When men are seen to be creatures of habit; yielding readily to sin; then man's estimate of man is at its lowest. It is when the master of self comes into view that man gets an adequate view of man. Because the tongue sends to the mind its appreciation of the sweet flavors of the world it has no right to say what the stomach will have put into it. Because the exercise of certain organs of man yield him pleasure they have no right to dictate to man the times when they shall be exercised. The man should not be a servant to his tastes and desires. Rather he should be master of all that goes to make up his being. It is when man stands up before us king of his own person, lord of himself, that we get the view and idea of him that we should have. Then we see him as he is capable of manifesting himself. Then we see him using the highest power he possesses, controlling the temporary form in order to keep wholesome the permanent life principle.

MAN'S GRADUAL REALIZATION OF HIS POWERS

CHAPTER IV

MAN'S GRADUAL REALIZATION OF HIS POWERS

THE Realization of man's powers was a slow process. The slowness of men in becoming perfectly self-controlled makes us say this. Primitive man, so far as we are able to judge from historical accounts that may be relied upon, revealed the basal powers of man, the ability to think, and the ability to put the thought into execution. He was placed in a world where every visible thing could be brought to serve him. Yet we find him rising very slowly from his primitive thoughts and acts. Each man to-day goes through this same stage of development. The thinking ability, though a part of the equipment from the beginning, has not been used to its full capacity at any time. The ability to do things, to act, though present from the first conscious moments, has never been exerted to the limit possible in any line of work. Every age shows an advance in the use of these faculties of man. Volumes have been written which tell us of the ever enlarging grasp of man, over the faculty of thought, and in the world of action. Yes, volumes will be written in the ages to come. And each will mark the expansion of a mind that we fain would say we know completely now.

The man who teaches his fellowmen how to use the faculty of thought must get of life the sweeter share. To have within one's hearing a group of men to whom the power of the mind and intellect is a sealed book, is to have within one's grasp the greatest opportunity that the world can offer. He is a dull teacher indeed who cannot make the blood tingle in the veins of such men. He is not in the right position, if in his own veins the blood does not run faster, when, for the first time, he opens up to the slumbering minds before him the vast possibilities of the thinking man.

He must have been the Supreme Power who could create a being as great as man is capable of being. The first man, like the new born babe, reveals but a part of what man as man has in him. A new creature in a new world would naturally seem crude and undeveloped. The marked progress from the first days reveals to us the innate power that was in man from the very beginning. He who could put into the original being the capacity for the thought and action seen in man to-day must have been a Wonderful Being indeed. A Being higher than any met in the experience of man upon earth. A Being who sums up in Himself more than the highest thought of man can attribute to Him. The ever constant increase in man's mind of the power to comprehend things that are, and the things that may be, would prompt the most conservative man to admit the truth of this.

It is almost impossible to think that man alone has been the cause of man's highest thought and action. The life, ordinarily lived by men whose minds have not been opened up, does not tend to make man attribute any such power as we have witnessed to the Life Giver. It is the highest type of man that causes us to have the highest conception of Him from whom all life came. The advance of man has been possible, in part, because of the inherent power in man. Nothing new, in the way of faculties or powers, is added to man's equipment during his earthly life. He develops the original gift. This he does by every aid that he can find. Nothing that he can do will give him any new power or faculty. He may wear an electric battery

on his person to stimulate the flow of blood, en-
abling him to continue his thinking beyond the
ordinary power of endurance, but had he not
in the beginning a mind capable of deep thought,
no amount of electric batteries would give it to
him. A man may take elements into his body to
stimulate his circulation of blood, thus making
it possible for him to pursue a protracted train
of reasoning, yet no one of these stimulants
could cause him to think, had he not the power
to think before he took the stimulant. The
germinal power came with man when he came.
It is not the possession of it that amazes us. The
ever increasing worth of the power holds our attention. There seems to be no limit fixed to the
development of this power. It is man's gift
from his Maker. It existed in germ in the first
man. To-day it has reached a high state in its
upward march to the Life Giver.

If this is so with the power of thought it is no
less so with the power of action. The prelimi-
nary actions of any creature are more crude
and reasonless than are the subsequent actions.
This applies to all animate creation. To-day
we look for a difference between the childhood
of a race and the maturity of the same. This
difference we expect to find in its thought and

in its action. Tribes or races, cannibalistic in tendency, coming in contact with forces that make them see the possibilities that lie in them and before them, leave their cannibalism on one side in their onward march of development. Could such tribes and races be kept free from the evil influences of corrupted wills the onward and upward march would know no check. It is when actors of decidedly bad parts come upon the scene, leading weak pupils astray, that we send up our cry for more men in the world whose purpose it is to do the acts that conform to the highest type of life known to man. It is when the non-thinking men become the leaders of those who should be taught the whole possibility of man that our cry goes up for more teachers and leaders of men from the class that has made most of the powers that are in man; from the class of men who count it a high privilege to put one soul on the path that leads to the highest development of self, on the path that will lead man to see between his Creator and himself a resemblance that maketh him not ashamed. There are men of the type mentioned. Their presence gives ground for the above. That more men have not developed to this point is in part the fault of the men who have. It is

true that no man can know any more than he is
willing to take into his mind. His teachers may
teach things that he does not know, but if he is
not sufficiently interested, the thing passes over
him and is lost to him. Given such a set of
men as pupils individual study will tell the thinking man that some key will open the mind of
every man present. Here is a truth that must
be placed in every mind before him. He goes
to work, ever varying his method, ever changing
his attack, until finally each man has seen the
thing the teacher would have him see. A man
who knows something that his brother ought to
know has not performed his duty until he has
shared the knowledge with his brother man.
The brother may not want the knowledge? He
may resent the attempts to teach him? Just so
much more difficult is the duty to be performed.
It remains a duty no matter how arduous it may
be made. The responsibility of telling rests upon those who know. This is a permanent responsibility. It remains just so long as any are
without the desired knowledge. Only those
who know can tell; only those who do not know
should persist in the minds of those who know.
If men of the highest intelligence, whose minds
are developed and raised to their highest power

do not feel the burden of raising the minds content with a lower state of power, then the minds not yet aware of their potential ability will come up accidentally at best. In them is the dormant power of development, it needs rousing. Only those who have waked up to the fact that mind must ever grow to come into its own, can arouse the sleeping ones. The Power that gave it to man could stir it up, but that is the unusual way of doing it. Human mind should be opened up by human mind. The rubbing together of human minds has brought about the great development of mind. Man must rub up against man, his idea being to develop self and the powers of self; and to do his part in the development of self in others.

ARE THERE CREATED BEINGS SUPE-RIOR TO MAN?

CHAPTER V

ARE THERE CREATED BEINGS SUPERIOR TO MAN?

PHILOSOPHY, as well as Biology, teaches us that life can come only from life. It also teaches us that the highest type of offspring cannot go above the highest type of progenitor. If these two propositions hold, and the world readily accepts them, then only one conclusion remains when considering animate creation. That conclusion is that there must have been a Being existing from all time who was capable of giving, or creating life. Having such a Being, with such Power, we have a cause sufficient to account for all the living creatures we see, or know to exist.

Man, being a product of the Life Giver, is subordinate to at least one Superior. Taking the visible world and its known creatures alone into consideration one would be tempted to say that there is no created being superior to man; and no Being superior to him save the Life Giver Himself. Man is the lord of all creation it seems; at least the Lord of the visible and tangible things known unto all.

Before you decide this matter of created beings superior to man, superior only because they are between man and the Life Giver, some thought is necessary. Having your study of man in the world, apart from the teachers of traditional beliefs, man is apt to find things that send his mind out in search of other forms of life not known definitely to man. It is not a strange sight, because it is not an infrequent sight, to see men of age and intelligence assembled together to receive what they call messages from the spirit world. For these people this world of spirits generally means the world that is made up of the spirits that have at some time inhabited human bodies, but which now are free from those bodies and make up the population of the place where such spirits go. The expression, however, "His good spirit has charge of him, preventing him from going astray," makes us feel that we cannot limit the spirit world to the souls only of those humans who have peopled the earth. We are led to think, because of the frequency of the above remark, that for each human soul there is another spirit or guide that never enters the world in flesh. This spirit has its sufficient part to play in aiding and assisting the soul it has been appointed to guide.

All this may come to us because of the traditional teaching of the highest civilization. But any
man in the world who makes an intimate study
of man would have this idea brought out in his
mind. He could see that life is the only thing
that can produce life. He would see that the
offspring does not excel the progenitor. And,
going back to the time when there was no living
creature upon earth, he would admit that some
life giving power must come in in order to cause
life to be in any created form. Having this power it would be seen that the variety of forms of
life depended wholly upon the will of the Power producing the life. Then that Power could
also say whether all the forms of life created
should be visible to all other forms of life or
not. In other words, admit a Giver of Life to
created forms, and you open up to any intelligent mind vast possibilities that go beyond any
form of being met with in man's experience.
You have also made possible the vast army of
spirits that would be needed by the Life Giving
Power, if He had willed that every human soul
should have its guardian spirit.

Man cannot say that he caused himself to exist. No man's earthly father can say it. Life
has its source not in man, but in a Being superior

to man, a Being who could put life into any object that He willed to see alive. The out and
out Evolutionist must admit that life had a beginning. He may not agree with the traditionalist that the various forms of life now seen and
known received instantaneously the gift of life.
His idea that all forms of life came from one
form of life may stand in his way. He must
admit that life had a beginning and development. He cannot deny the statement that life
comes only from life. So the evolutionist is
brought to a point where he must agree with the
traditionalist in saying, that there is a Being
from whom the first spark of life, as we know it,
came, He who put into the form created the
germinant power. The men who think agree in
this: that the life we know had its source in a
higher life that we do not fully know. At this
time it matters little what the Giver of life as
we know it may be called. Even a hasty view of
man would compel a thinker to attribute great
power to the Being capable of producing man.
The man who loves to study would be forced
to take time to consider the nature of the Being
who could put into existence the involved being
known to man as man. One of the things that
we could expect from the thinking would be

this. The Being performing such a great work must have been capable of performing a greater work, and must still be able to repeat all that He has ever done. He did not give to man all of His power, for man cannot give independent life to inanimate objects. The Life Giver did not exhaust Himself in the work of giving life to created forms; He gives life in the same way to-day. (It is one of the accepted views of the highest civilization that every man born into the world alive has had placed in the formed body, by the power of the Life Giver, that spark which animates the product of male and female.)

Having such a Power as the source of our life we can easily see the possibility of other forms of life not yet met with in our experience. The man who believes in guardian spirits, creatures as we are of the Life Giver, created for the definite work that he believes they do, must be allowed his belief. It is a possible presumption. And if the Source of Life be good in character and intent, the above is a probable method adopted to bring man to the Life Giver's thought and habit. As a belief it must be granted to man. The very presence in the world of man, with the vast powers that he reveals, makes highly probable the existence of beings not now known to man. Should the Life Giver, He who caused to be all that we see, be tied down in His plan or work by the limits experienced by a part of His creation?

MAN THE FINAL ARBITER OF HIS OWN ACTIONS

CHAPTER VI

MAN THE FINAL ARBITER OF HIS OWN ACTIONS

WERE a man to tell you that you were bound to do everything which you did, that no other course was open to you, it was absolutely necessary that you did thus and so, you would feel like telling that man that he knew nothing about the matter. There are few things harder to believe to-day than the statement that man is necessarily bound to a certain course of conduct; i. e. the one that he pursues. It is quite easy to believe any scientific fact that comes to us through authoritative channels. We take the statements of astronomical authorities when there is not the least possible chance to verify their statements. We believe accounts found in ordinary newspapers when they tell us of feats in air, in sea, or on land. Our credulity seems unlimited, yet when a man tells us that we are merely running and acting in a groove, out of which we cannot get, we, at the moment, have presumption enough to tell that man that he knows no more about it than we do.

We should not turn hastily from the man who thinks differently from us. He may have seen a truth that has escaped us. It seems reasonable to suppose that the founder of all life would be able to outline a course for His created life to run. It is possible for Him to do what He pleases with His creation. Had the Life Giver mapped out the life of each of the human beings to whom He gave the breath of life, He would have been doing just the thing to fit in with the ideas that some men have of a giver of life. There are men who think that all that they create, or make, belongs to them individually to do with as they will. They cannot see that if their creation is to be of benefit to all mankind it should be given to all mankind without restriction. They retain by patent or copyright their control over the child of their powers. So they follow it to the grave, until it is buried by reason of some other man's superior creation. To men of this class it is an easy step from human creation and control to Divine Creation and Control. The author and maker is the guide and finisher. The Being, creating forms and giving life to them, ordains for each a certain task in a certain place. Should an individual worker jump to the farthest point in

the world from that in which the work was be-
gun, he did it because the Power that gave him
his being ordered it. This whole plan seems
reasonable enough; it is possible. The Giver of
Life, in that He made possible the life of the
individual human being, revealed to the world
the fact that He had sufficient power to rule and
guide human beings. But does an intimate study
of man make anyone really believe that the Life
Giver is controlling the actions of men?

When you see masses of men banded together in order that other men may be employed at
the smallest possible wage, and made to labor
the longest possible number of hours a day, do
you feel that He, who first introduced life upon
earth, no matter what you may think of Him
as to His character as a whole, planned that
men should so act against men? When you
see, multitudes of indolent and shiftless men at-
tacking with stones and staves other men who
are trying to earn honestly enough money to
keep their families alive, do you think that these
men are obeying any other being than themselves? There are in the world many men
whose study is not what it should be. Men and
money get together daily, but men fail to study
one as much as they do the other. If men would

study how to make men as much as they study how to make money, there would not be so many brands of socialism in the world. All men would be of the same brand. They would study on one side the multitudes that seek a living wage; they would study on the other side the men capable of paying this wage. Such study would eventuate in a better understanding, a higher ground for the settlement needed, and a happier issue than the world has as yet seen.

Looking at things as they are we see too much of the lower nature of man revealed in the world to prompt us to believe that man is but following out a plan of life laid down by the Life Giver. The contraries of human life must be explained on a different basis too. The man who kills his brother man in a brawl brought on by a discussion over a strike, is seen a few moments later giving his last crust of bread to the starving child of his loins. We can readily see that man has a better nature; the occasional ruling of that better nature gives us a picture of life different from that which we most frequently get. We think back to the time when the first man stood before his Maker. Man then had in him a part of the Life Giver. If he had it then he has it now. Suppose that the Life Giver had decided to control man's actions in the world, would they conform to the better nature of man or to the lower nature, the bad nature? To answer this definitely man has to take another critical look into man to see if there is in his make-up that thing which we call bad. Is man bad, or only capable of becoming so?

One does not have to look back far in the history of the world to come into contact with man almost as he was when he had placed in him the breath of life by the Life Giver. The American Indian, before he came in contact with the white man, was a good man. His habits of life were clean, this is made evident to-day in the manly characters still found among the remnant. But go among the remnant of some of the tribes and examine the younger generation. You will find male and female debased in thought, word and deed. You will find a diseased, shiftless, and sorrowful lot, not reflecting credit upon man or his country. Yet they are the same Indians, capable of the same wild, open, and free life of yesterday. They are the same kind of men and women that found pleasure in the life of nature, free from the wiles of men. The evil desires, the evil thoughts, the evil deeds, these are the dregs of civilization, carried among

them by men of bad wills. These things have
made the Indian seem a despicable creature. The
"bad Indian" of to-day is a sign and token of
the work of men who were controlled by nothing else than their love for the things of the
lower nature of man. On one Reservation, in
a supposedly civilized State, every crime com-
mitted in recent years has been traced back to its
inception; and strong drink, introduced into the
Reservation by characterless white men, has
been found responsible in every instance.

Man, kept apart from the evil wills of the
world of men, is given to good thoughts and
deeds. If man in his own self is such, is it not
permissible to imagine his Sender-into-the-world
to be of like character? Imagining Him to be
the same, would it not be probable that, if He
were to keep the controlling hand in man's life,
He would have that life reveal its best thoughts,
words, and deeds? The highest type of life
that man was capable of living?

The possibility in every man to become good,
to do every day the actions that show no ill-will,
vindictive spirit, corrupt mind, would cause us,
if we allowed it to do so, to say that there are
no really bad men in the world. Those whom
we call bad, because of their infraction of laws

written or unwritten, are men, who, for the moment, obey an impulse that is not in harmony with their real self. If man cannot obey the good impulse, is bound to obey the bad impulse, then there is no such thing as virtue in the world; we are all actors, playing our several parts until the curtain takes us from the public gaze. Give a man the power to choose the way he shall go, the particular part he shall play to-day, and every day; then you have a man to whom you may impute goodness or badness as his chosen part may warrant. The good man, to whom no other way was open, cannot be called such by right. You may as well call it a virtue in the binder, when every day it so beautifully ties up the cut sheaves of grain. The creator of it made it possible for it to do this work well. It does it. It cannot do anything else; there is no choice for it. No man would ascribe virtue to such a machine. No more would the man who is called good deserve the title, if it were impossible for him to be anything else. The man who commits sins, or crimes, should not be punished for such things, if he could not choose the path that led away from such deeds. The whole system of jurisprudence is built up upon the idea that man may do, or he may not do, a given thing appearing in his mind. Make man a marionette, with some invisible hand pulling the strings that make him act, and you have taken away from man the very power upon which rest all the reasons for human or Divine laws.

When a man tells us that our actions are all planned beforehand by the Power that caused us to be, we do well if we talk reasonably with him on the subject. If there are beings of a higher order than man, they may be endued with a power of influence that can be exerted upon man. If this power is exerted upon man, in order that man may be led to do certain things, in preference to other contemplated things, then there is another foundation reason for the man who believes that our lives are planned by a Power above us. Yet this reason is not sufficient to support his whole belief. To get a base that will support his entire faith we must say point blank that the Power that made us is still claiming ownership, and still exacting royalty; just the same as human beings do who are intelligent enough to discover some new way to make shoes with less expense, or to invent some new machine that will put the finished product of the cotton field upon the market quicker, cheaper, and better than in the old way. We are creations of a Mind, and that Mind must control our actions. This seems to be the logic of the case.

No one would deny that the possibility exists in the Giver of Life to enter at any moment and change, if He so desired, the mode of life of the beings to whom He had given life. Nor could any one, admitting His power to cause life to be, deny His incidental power to influence the life that He has created. If the life came from Him, it would seem natural that He still has the power to direct, if He so chose, the life which He had created. This gives us only an influence in the life of man, not a compelling force that cannot be resisted. Yet, were we pressed by our friend who thinks that all men are controlled in life by a Power above them, controlled so firmly that while they seem to have a choice of two ways that lie before them, they really have no such choice, we could not deny the possibility of such a thing when we think of the power that must be possessed by the Being who could introduce the life we see into a lifeless world.

It is chiefly the fact that man does the evil instead of the good, works the works of the flesh instead of the good works of the heart and soul, that we say that man is ruler of himself.

He wills to do a certain thing and he does it.
He feels that he may do it or leave it undone,
just as he chooses. As man studies man there
is no principle that becomes so firmly fixed in his
mind as this one:—man may be master of himself every conscious minute of his life upon
earth. He is the one from whom every member
of his body takes orders. If the order is to dis-
obey man's law, the law is disobeyed. If the
order is to live in peace and harmony with all
mankind, the order is obeyed. There are
forces working upon man that cannot be seen,
forces that cause him to change his course daily.

"We see not half the causes of our deeds,
Seeking them wholly in the outer life,
And heedless of the encircling spirit world
Which, though unseen, is felt, and sows in us
All germs of pure and world-wide purposes."

No matter what it is that causes man to alter his
course, to choose this way rather than the other,
it is man who changes the course. He may resist to the last all the forces and influences, he
may run his course without yielding to any outside thing or power. Man has the final say
in every action; when a man acts it is because he
himself has willed to do so.

MAN'S OBLIGATION

MAN'S OBLIGATION.

CHAPTER VII

MAN'S OBLIGATION

IT does not take long for a thinking man to see that he is powerless, in his own strength to provide for his own needs. The owner of the great western farm, who tills the soil, and sows the seed, has not the power to bring the seed to fruition. He knows not which of his fields is to bring forth the expected crop. He may irrigate the soil, thus giving to the young shoot that which it needs to keep life in it. He may, artificially, cause light and heat to lend their aid in the battle for life and results. But the seed has many moments between seed time and harvest time of which the farmer knoweth not. There are moments when the sower will give up all hope of reaping any harvest. A short time later he finds that he did not know the hidden power of the seed, the soil, and the Giver of Power to both.

Man, in his infancy, imagines that it is by his ✓ own right hand or by the cunning of his brain that he lives. At this stage his mind has not come into its own. The man is yet untutored in the world of realities. When his mind is doing its full work, taking into it and turning over in it all the things that it may, then man comes to a different conclusion. Then it is that he finds he is dependent upon a force outside of himself. If he be anxious to increase his knowledge, his own worth to himself and to his fellowman, he will pursue his study of man's dependence. He will say, "This force outside of me which aids the work I do in the fields is, or is not, due to previous arrangement of Him who gave me life." Upon investigation it is found that all of the needs of created beings are arranged for, in order that the life given to them may be sustained. The man then readily sees that only a Mind acquainted with the needs of all created life could so adequately provide for those needs. And to the Supreme Being, who caused the first life to be upon the earth, he ascribes a mind of like character to his own. If the Supreme Being is wise enough to provide for all of man's physical needs, and the physical needs of all created life, He would not be the Being above all others should He stop with this. Having provided the means by which the life given might be sustained, He would surely have, in His own Mind at least, a plan of life for all of His created beings.

Can we find such a plan in our study of man?

If any plan of life is in the Mind of the Life Giver for the created beings that man knows, it must be found in the world and in man. Go into a section of your city inhabited by the poorest and the most ignorant. As you walk through the unfamiliar streets, and meet the unfamiliar faces, you are tempted to feel that this part of your city has no part or place in your life. You walk hurriedly by the squalid scenes. Perhaps you draw your coat closely about you lest it touch any of the wretched beings in your path. Should you by chance meet an acquaintance while on this visit you are put to it to account for your presence there. There is apt to be a feeling in your mind that makes you think you are not one with the people you have seen. That the scenes you witnessed have nothing to do with your life. The whole thing must pass from you as a horrible night-mare. Despite this feeling on your part you are one with the worst type of man that you have beheld. The revolting scenes that you have witnessed are as much a part of your life as they are a part of the life of those directly involved in them.

Human life came from a common source. Any being that reveals the inherent powers of

man is potentially the equal of the highest type
of man. Where do we learn this? By a study
of man as he is. We find that all men are brothers because of the common Father, or Source of
human life. Being brothers it is the duty of
man to be brotherly to all mankind. This means
that the squalid tenement and its unclean inhab-
itants mean something to every man. The feeling which we have when we view the poor side
of human existence does not become us unless it
be a brotherly feeling. · If there is the least
trace of aloofness in spirit, "these people are too
wretched, these conditions too squalid for my
presence," then we are not yet ready to go to
such places or to meet such people. The man
who imagines that birth, position, wealth, or
any other human thing sets him up above his fellowmen, is not yet fit to mingle among men. He
is fit only for a solitary seat, where, unmolested
by lesser beings, he may feast upon his own vir-
tues. As a leader of men he cannot be successful for he can bring men only to his own level.
Beyond a certain point he cannot lead them or
direct them. And such a man will be content to
make copies of himself. The man who has
realized the fact that no human thing makes one
man of greater worth than another, in the sight

of Him who caused man to be, is the man who can direct men on beyond the position which he himself holds. Weaknesses may prevent him from ascending the heights that are in his vision. He has the power to show his brothers the way, and he has the will to wish that his brothers may reach the heights. Considering himself one of the many among whom he finds himself daily, he is able, by reason of his lack of self exaltation, to win men to a life different from the life to which they have been devoting themselves.

There is another trait in man that prevents him from benefiting other men, or being benefited himself by his contact with other men. That trait is called selfishness. It may be described by the phrases—"All for self and nothing for others." It is a trait seen in every day life, and in every section of life. No place, no matter how high in life's station the people congregating there may be, is free from this trait of selfishness. It makes one man send another to the poorhouse. It makes one man send another man to the penitentiary. It makes one man drive another man to suicide and the grave. It is a relic of barbarism, of the time when a man's life was worth only the material things which he possessed. This is the trait in man that

prompts one to use that grinding process by
which the very soul of another is torn beyond
all recognition. It is man's trait, prompting
him to reveal the truth in the much worn phrase
—"The survival of the fittest."

This character is not the thinker. He is not
the man who has found, by contact with man,
his duty to man. One, with this trait prominent,
has not been looking for the obligation that rests
upon him to treat all mankind as brothers. He
has been, and is, too busy exacting his rights to
think of his duties. It is given only to the man
who seeks, to find. It is he who starts out with
a strong purpose to know something about the
things that may be known who gets the knowledge. There must be *willingness* to understand
before a man *can* understand. The selfish man
changes his part only when deep in his heart is
the desire to know and help other men. The
greatest joy that comes to the worker among
men is the knowledge that he gains; making him
see the possibility, inherent even in a selfish man,
to change almost instantly from his old self to
a being with love and care for his brother man.
The old phrase changes to this—"The survival
of all by the aid of the fittest." Then you have
a whole creation, so far as man is concerned,

not a divided or split one. You have one man working for another man because they are parts of the same whole. You have in man a keen feeling that only by such thought and work for others can the obligation that rests upon him be met. The man possessing the most must share with him who possesses the least. The man who is strongest must help the man who is weakest; that the whole human army may present as strong a front as is possible; revealing in a united and harmonious whole the plan of life ordained by the Giver of Life. Not only should man live and let live,—that is but a step in the sphere of selfishness,—he should add to this good will his assisting power. Not merely refusing to resist the efforts of others to live and prosper, but actively helping the others to attain the good things which they seek. This is the step out of the realm of selfishness into the sphere of usefulness. This step makes man a co-worker with the Giver of Life, in that he is helping to perpetuate the life given. He is also calling attention to the fact that the life given was meant to be a life of service to others and not a life devoted to self. Those who see this as the plan of life for human beings, and follow it, because it seems that it must be the plan of the Supreme

Being, reap a thousand fold where formerly they viewed barren fields. The joy of man when he gets fully in touch with man is a joy that is not easily given up or taken away.

It is renewed day by day, it is sufficient reward for acquiescing in the life plan for human beings ordained by the Life Giver. It is the highest plan that man can find in the world of man, it must therefore have some relation to the plan that the Supreme Being would formulate, were He to formulate one. Man's obligation is to find out the highest plan of life and to adopt it as his own; the plan of life that takes into consideration the whole body of human beings and not the detached parts or sections; the plan that tells man what he must do for others as well as what he may do for himself.

UPON WHAT DOES MAN'S OBLIGATION REST?

CHAPTER VIII

Upon What Does Man's Obligation Rest?

THE man who thinks will admit that there is an obligation resting upon him to pursue a certain line of conduct in the world. Put the idea to a man who has not realized the highest powers of his being and he may try to evade the necessity of such obligation. Only the fullest realization of self can put a man in the position to get the correct view of life. As long as a man is deficient in any stage of self-development just so long is he incapable of getting the right viewpoint of life. He will cling to the idea, unless he comes to a knowledge of the full content of self, that life is only an opportunity for him to provide for his own needs and pleasures, and the needs and pleasures of his blood and flesh successors. When man continues to provide unnecessary luxuries for his immediate dependents, without giving a thought or a deed that would assist the needy in securing necessities, we may be sure that that man is not yet aware of the obligation resting upon all mankind. Like

the horse and the mule that man must be driven,
if he is to do the right thing. Unlike horse and
mule he may come to a point where the right
thing may be done because of his own volition.
Creatures without understanding cannot be expected to do the right thing all the time. Beings with understanding may be expected to do
what is right all the time, when the understanding is awakened. Man has a definite obligation
resting upon him in this life. That obligation
is based upon the fact that all mankind pro-
ceeds from a common source. To the Supreme
Being who gave life to the world all must look
for the power that enables man to be, to think,
and to do.

Two brothers of one earthly father may not
be congenial to each other. Instead of growing
up together in peace and concord they grow up
apart from each other in thought and deed,
making wider the gulf between them year by
year. All this because the temperament of one
differs from the temperament of the other.
There is no effort made by either brother to
reconcile the differences that exist. The old
spirit of selfishness comes in to aid in the family
separation. One must have his way and desires,
the other is just as determined to have his way

and desires. The result is that the potentially united whole, the family, becomes a hard hearted group of individuals.

Take one of these unawakened sons and put him into juxtaposition with other young men, not as congenial as his own brother was even, and, human nature is so capricious, you soon find him on the best of terms with them. Being thrown together in such a way that it was necessary to get the other men's points of view, there comes a time when the other men are admitted to friendship and respect, though the possibility of such a termination seemed highly improbable at the start.

If one could get the two uncongenial sons together after several such experiences on each one's part, it ought to be an easy matter to bring them together in heart as well as in space. That old appeal ought to sound reasonable in their ears, namely, that the sons of the same earthly father ought to make more allowances for each other than they make for the sons of other earthly fathers. Having in each the blood of the same parents they are more one with each other than they can be with any other earthly being. The fact that they both came out of the same loins ought to make them feel that they would

give up even their very life for each other. After
all this you could tell them that the common
parent deserves some recognition in such a case.
Man, when considering self alone, is apt to do
many things that he would not do, if he took
into consideration all those human beings who
are to be affected by his contemplated act.   It
is patent to every man that every other man has,
in part at least, the same desires, feelings, and
powers as himself.   Action in the world of man
is often so hasty that man has no time to think
of the feeling that his acts will cause in the minds
of others.   So when you get the uncongenial
brothers to look from themselves to the common parent, to consider his feelings in the case,
to allow for his claim, you ought to be nearing
the end of your work as peacemaker.   The time
should be at hand when, for the sake of *all concerned*, the uncongenial ones will live together in
love and sympathy.

The obligation upon man to show this same
love and sympathy to all men, regardless of their
condition or position in life, rests upon the feeling that we think must be in the Mind of the
Being great enough to make man as he is capable of being.   If the fact that every man is our
brother, because of a common source of life, be

not sufficient to move us to do unto all men as we are willing and anxious to do for ourselves, then the other thought must be urged in our endeavor to secure for every man the love and help of every other man. If our earthly fathers are grieved and sorrow stricken because of the estrangements of their sons, is it unreasonable to suppose that He, who caused all created forms to be, and put into them the life which we see, is affected sadly by the gulfs that yawn between men in this world? Is the Life Giver to blame because the untutored savage is untutored? Is He to blame for the multitudes of people in this fair land of ours who know not their own powers, nor the Power that made them and us? Ignorant men are ignorant because they will to be so, or because intelligent men do not will it to be otherwise. As long as intelligent men think that a gift of their time now and then for the purpose of attending to the education of the ignorant is sufficient, just so long will the ignorant remain so. As long as men with material resources think that an occasional gift of money makes evident to the world their due care for their less favored brothers, just so long will the less favored remain so. The intelligent must give themselves

to the work. The men with the material resources must likewise give themselves. Unless
the heart of both classes of men is in it, the
work will never be done. That any time or
money is given for the purpose of bringing the
ignorant to a knowledge of things as they are,
is a cause for thankfulness. It shows that many
men recognize the obligation that rests upon all
mankind. The fact that the problem is not attacked, as many problems of less importance are
attacked, is a sign that man has not yet yielded
himself to the will of the Supreme Being. What
has been done seems to have been the efflux of
individuals when their own needs or desires have
been satisfied.

The fact that all life comes from the same
source, thus making brothers of all human beings, is not sufficient to impel man to do his full
duty to his brother man. If the brother is congenial, the duty may be done. If the fulfilling
of the duty promises to be at all distasteful, it is
apt to be left undone. The obligation is re-
garded and lived up to, if the tax is not too
great. Thus far and no farther will the ordinary man go. This attitude is too common in
the world for any one to deny its presence.
When a man is found who really wishes to

know the highest good it is a comparatively easy thing to make him see that such a state of affairs is not the state any being, allowing the better nature to rule, would deliberately plan. It is not the plan followed by individuals when serving their country as soldiers. In that service a man will cast himself to instant death at the bidding of a man who stands as his superior in the eyes of his country. A man will also give himself to death in order that a college or university may hang upon its walls a certain football trophy. Both of these men may have refused to speak a kind word to their mother at no far remote date. Not one of these acts are the acts to be expected from man in his highest state of intelligence.

The obligation that is upon man to treat all other men with love and sympathetic consideration is based finally upon the highly probable fact that the One who gave us a common life desires us to do so. After trial it is found to be the best attitude that man can take toward man. It accords with all that is best in man. It seems to be the result of the highest intelligence in man. It must be potential in every man receiving the gift of life. If we may attribute to the Life Giver the same powers that man possesses, and

He must have known about them or have had them, in order to place them in man, then He must rejoice, as our highest intelligences rejoice, when one man is seen to come to a point where he gets a clearer view of human life, and sees it as it should be lived by man among men. It must be the Supreme Being's aim, as it should be the aim of every intelligent man upon earth, to make more men, and more men, until the last are reached, see and know this life of love and good will among men; in order that the sons of one Father may be one family, united in the great bond of sympathy and love; in order that all those, deriving life from the great Life Giver, may be of service to the common source of their life by bringing up to the highest level of human life those capable of reaching it, but who are held down by self or environment.

MAN'S TRUE GOAL

CHAPTER IX

Man's True Goal

WHEN man ceases to be man by reason of the separation of the visible body and that which has animated the body, there is not found in the minds and hearts of those persons to whom the man in point was dear, a sadness that has no ray of light. This fact can be seen in all records that speak of such an event. It is not a traditional fact of only nineteen hundred years standing, it is a fact of ages upon ages. Man cannot live in the world even a short time without having this strange fact brought to his mind. There is sorrow when the familiar form becomes inanimate, but the sorrow is not a perpetual sorrow, it is a sorrow for a night only. Even on the day that sees the separation of form and its vital part there comes to the eye of those to whom the form and life were dear, a look that tells of something beside sorrow.

Almost every other thing we have considered in our time together is common only to those who have advanced somewhat in the ways open to man. This thing, this consciousness of a look ahead when a dear form and its life principle are separated, is common to all men. The poor, the rich, the ignorant, and the intelligent, when standing at the door through which the departed life has gone, all have the same thought, the same hope. It matters not what each has been taught or how much; teaching, or its lack, has nothing to do with this idea that lives within us, as to its inception. It seems to be a part of the original gift of the Life Giver. True it is that no man has been found, standing at the brink of the opened grave, forced to part forever with the loved form, who has not had within him the means of quieting his grief. His desire to have the form animate again may prevent him from allowing the inner solace to do its appointed work. He has the idea; it is as universal as the life principle which we reveal to the world when we act. It could not be so universal unless it were placed in man when man was made a living being. It is a hope, felt strongly enough at times to seem to be a reality, that somewhere, somehow, the living, thinking, acting part of man will continue, after it is separated from the form to which it has given a use, to be alive, and to think, and to act.

There is only one kind of life that would be endurable throughout all time. That is the best life, the cleanest life, the life dictated by the highest that is in man. A life in which the misunderstandings of this life would be done away. Where justice would be dealt out to those who had suffered injustice in this world. And thus it is that the separation of the life from the form often makes a man who suffers the loss take more thought to his own ways than he formerly took. There is a feeling which tells him that only those who make the life lived agree with the highest life possible will merit a revision of judgment, the removal of limitations. When man is called upon to part with some loved one because the time has come for the separation of the life and the form, it is a common sight to see him go out into the world, and, in a bungling sort of way, attempt to do something to show a friendly feeling toward equally sorrowing humanity. At that moment man feels the claim of universal brotherhood whether he is an ignorant or an educated man. One little drop of human kindness at such a time, the acceptance of the assistance offered, may be the cause of sending out into the world an agent of the right life, a man imbued with the spirit that must have been in Him who gave life to all created forms.

When a man loves anything with all his heart and soul he does not wish ever to be separated from the object of his love. Have you not heard of men who made it a part of their last message to human beings in this world that their bodies be wrapped in a certain piece of bunting, called a flag? This is a case where man makes an incident in his earthly life the ruling thing in his life. He may have borne arms under that flag. Arms that were made for the quicker separation of form and life; that were made for the sole purpose of extinguishing the life which a Common Life Giver had given to all living beings. The bearing and using of such arms could not give man cause to be proud, if he considered the matter when his highest powers were in control of his mind and action. Yet the flag that brought back all the memories of heroic deeds, the risking of life in order to take life from other men, this flag must go with the body to the grave. It is well that no one asks to have the flag wrapped around the life principle. Its flight back to its Giver could not be hailed with joy should it appear wearing the badge of the enemy of life. The flag is wrapped, as it should be, about the perishable part of man, the form

that the Life Giver made for the revealing of
the life, showing to all who gaze that it too belongs to the fleeting things of time.

If a man is going to love anybody or thing
with all his heart and soul, it seems reasonable
to ask him to bestow such love on the Source of
his being. If a man's life is a gift from a definite Source, that Source is worthy of recognition
by man. Especially is this so if the life has
proved itself to be of worth. Man generally,
always when "in his right mind," regards his
life as worth a great deal. This being so it be-
hooves him, before he sets his affections completely upon lesser things, to find out all he can
about the Source of his and every life. It is only
because men do not think that they become so at-
tached to transitory things. It is the first impulse that is obeyed, there is no waiting to thor-
oughly examine all claims that come before the
throne of individual man. Those who think,
who use the powers of man to the limit, come to
a point where they have to set their affections
upon the Source of all life or upon themselves.
There are no other alternatives for the man
who uses his mind as it should be used. He
comes to a point where he must worship either
the creature or the Creator. The larger num-

ber of these thinking men take the Creator for the object of worship. It seems to them a foolish thing to fall down and adore a power that equals only the power of man, when a greater Power may be sought and known. The greater Power rightly deserves the greater consideration. "We needs must love the highest when we see it."

What would this greater Power have those who think of Him and love Him do? Reasoning from the life of man to the life of Him who made man a living being, we would be tempted to say that the highest joy the Creator could have would be the joy that would come to Him when all of the human beings, to whom He had given life, came back to Him, revealing the highest powers and qualities of which they were capable. The man who sends his offspring out into the world to make his way in that world is filled with great joy when that offspring comes back glowing with manly vigor and evident virtue. The heart of the earthly parent goes up when the word comes that the son has played the man so successfully that the world of men applaud. Contrary feelings come when the offspring has brought disgrace upon the name of man. May we attribute such feelings to Him from whom all life came? If we may, is it not man's true goal to go back to the Source of his being every bit a man? May we not picture to man the Life Giver as a Being so vitally interested in man's pilgrimage through this world that He will hail with joy the completion of the journey when it has been a successful journey? May we not picture the Life Giver as a loving Father waiting anxiously for the return of each son?

Were man content to aim at reaching this goal alone he would not be a whole man. In the world of men, to men are entrusted the safety and well being of other men. There are guides who know ways unknown to ordinary men. To these men is given the privilege of conducting other men to the goal that they would or should reach. If it is a good for any human being to strive to go back to the Creator whole in every respect, it undoubtedly is a good to be the means of bringing back to the Creator a human being who knew Him not as the Source of being, or knowing Him as such, had not the power alone to get back to Him.

Were an earthly parent aware of the fact that two of his sons in a far off country, trying to make men of themselves, were assisting one another in the battle, the stronger one always helping the weaker one, the knowledge must please him. If the coming back to the earthly parent depended upon the accomplishment of a certain amount of work, or in being a certain kind of man, it must please the parent were he to know that the one who had fulfilled the requirements was delaying his home coming in order to make possible the bringing of his brother with him. For the natural father loves all of his sons with the same intensity.

May we attribute the same feeling to the Source of life? May we urge men to be whole men because of the joy such wholeness will cause in Him who made it possible for us to be such men? Can man have a higher aim in life than this? To be whole, complete in every part, and to help other men realize in themselves this same wholeness, this same completeness? In order that the life principle, returning to Him who gave it, may report the attainment of its highest possibilities!

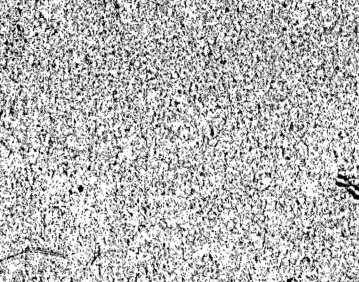

SD - #0037 - 010222 - C0 - 229/152/6 - PB - 9780259430452 - Gloss Lamination